Day Trading Forex

Escape the 9 to 5 and Retire Early: Learn Essential Forex Day Trading Skills. Currency Trading Explained in Simple Terms. Tools, Software, Tactics, Money Management, Discipline, Strategies and Trading Psychology

© Copyright 2017 by William B. McGuigan- All rights reserved.

The following book is reproduced below with the goal of providing information that is as accurate and as reliable as possible. Regardless, purchasing this book can be seen as consent to the fact that both the publisher and the author of this book are in no way experts on the topics discussed within, and that any recommendations or suggestions made herein are for entertainment purposes only. Professionals should be consulted as needed before undertaking any of the action endorsed herein.

This declaration is deemed fair and valid by both the American Bar Association and the Committee of Publishers Association and is legally binding throughout the United States.

Furthermore, the transmission, duplication or reproduction of any of the following work, including precise information, will be considered an illegal act, irrespective whether it is done electronically or in print. The legality extends to creating a secondary or tertiary copy of the work or a recorded copy and is only allowed with the express written consent of the Publisher. All additional rights are reserved.

The information in the following pages is broadly considered to be a truthful and accurate account of facts, and as such any inattention, use or misuse of the information in question by the reader will render any resulting actions solely under their purview. There are no scenarios in which the publisher or the original author of this work can be in any fashion deemed liable for any hardship or damages that may befall them after undertaking information described herein.

Additionally, the information found on the following pages is intended for informational purposes only and should thus be considered, universal. As befitting its nature, the information presented is without assurance regarding its continued validity or interim quality. Trademarks that mentioned are done without written consent and can in no way be considered an endorsement from the trademark holder.

Table of Contents

Introduction 1

Chapter 1: Forex Trading Defined 3

Chapter 2: Understanding Market Trends 10

Chapter 3: Frequently-Used Terminology on the Foreign-Exchange Market 18

Chapter 4: Common Chart Patterns You're Likely to See . 29

Chapter 5: The Attitude You Need to Cultivate 37

Chapter 6: Beginner Strategies to Make You a Buck 44

Chapter 7: Online Tools Every New Forex Trader Should Use 52

Chapter 8: Three Different Forex Markets from Which You Can Trade 61

Chapter 9: All About Stop Loss Orders 67

Chapter 10: How to Manage Your Risk Like a Winner 72

Conclusion 78

Introduction

Congratulations on purchasinging your personal copy of Day Trading Forex : Escape the 9 to 5 and Retire Early: Learn Essential Forex Day Trading Skills. The Basics of Currency Trading Explained in Simple Terms. Tools, Software, Tactics, Money Management, Discipline, Strategies, and Trading Psychology. Thank you for doing so.

The following chapters are going to discuss everything that you need to learn about becoming an investor in the Forex trading market. We will cover learning Forex basics in simple terms so that you can easily understand and use otherwise complex jargon and Forex trading techniques in your own life. After we've gone over the basic terms surrounding Forex investment trading and what Forex trading is, we will then move into understanding strategies that you can implement in order to take your investment money and grow more of it. As with any type of investment strategy, learning the basics first is the only way to truly master more complex later one.

In addition to learning about some beginner strategies to have under your belt, this book will also get into some of the best software and other learning tools that exist for someone who is new to Forex trading. This way, you will be able to practice trading on this type of market. This will likely prevent you from losing your shirt when you eventually do decide to start trading on the Forex market in real time.

There are plenty of books on this subject on the market, thanks again for choosing this one! Every effort was made to ensure it is full of as much useful information as possible, please enjoy!

Chapter 1

Forex Trading Defined

One of the most important aspects of any type of investment strategy is understanding the market on which you're going to be trading. That's why this chapter is important. While you do not necessarily need to understand how the Forex market came to be in order to trade on this platform, having as much information as possible regarding this market is only going to enhance your experience as someone who is looking to reap a profit. This chapter is going to discuss what Forex trading is, and why it matters in our global economy today. After reading this chapter, you will have a complete grasp on how various economies throughout the world interact with one another, and why this interaction is important.

The Forex Market

The term Forex is actually an abbreviated conjunction. When separated, Forex can be broken into two words, Foreign Exchange. Known for being one of the most volatile and therefore exciting markets on which investors can trade, the Forex market is largely unmonitored, especially when compared to other types of stock markets that exist. Additionally, unlike other types of markets that open and close at a certain time, the Forex market only rest for about forty hours per week. This is because the Forex market deals with many different time zones simultaneously. This fact can sometimes be seen as a disadvantage to investors because it means that the potential is there for you to literally lose money while you're sleeping.

The Call for All Currencies to be Equal

If you've ever traveled to another country and have had to convert your currency to the currency of that other country, then you already have a basic idea of how the Forex market operates. You see, instead of dealing with stocks, bonds, or mutual funds, the Forex market is all about trading currency in the form of an exchange rate. It's very unlikely that two currencies from two different countries would ever possess the exact same value. This is why an exchange rate exists. The Forex market is able to facilitate the ability of people from different countries to have a stake in each other's economies, political events, and other aspects of socio-political life.

A Disseminate Market

We can all probably conjure an image in our head of the floor at the New York Stock Exchange. This floor is constantly littered with investors day in and day out who seem to be constantly shouting in order to solidify deals for their clients. The Forex market is nothing like this. Instead of being a centrally-controlled entity, the Forex market is what's known as a disseminate market. This means that authority is dispersed throughout the world. From a global perspective, this makes sense. If only one country were controlling the flow of money on an international market, it can be argued that the global nature of the market itself would be compromised.

It's important to understand that disseminate does not mean ungoverned. The Forex market should not be regarded as a free-for-all zone where anything goes. Each country that is represented on the Forex is governed by an entity that is distinct to its own country. For example, in the United States, this entity is known as the Commodities Futures Trading Commission of the United States. In China, it's known as SAFE, or the State Administration of Foreign Exchange. Due to the decentralized nature of the Forex, it's advised that you read up on the regulations in both the country in which you're trading as well as the country in which you're seeking to negotiate.

What Type of Currency Is Traded?

There are over one-hundred types of currency that are traded in the world today (officially), but most payments in the world right now are done using the US dollar, the Japanese Yen, and the European euro. The Swedish krona, the Canadian dollar, the Swiss franc, and the British pound are all also popular currency types following the first three. In thinking about the relevance of certain types of currency, it can help to contextualize why the Forex market matters. The fact of the matter is that not all currency is created equal. Some currency is regarded more highly than others. Even though this is the case, people who traded all types of currency are able to convert their currency into other types, due to the exchange rates that the Forex offers. In this way, people are able to interact more freely within a global context.

Commercial Trade versus Speculative Trade

There are two types of transactions that primarily take place within Forex. These are known as commercial trades and speculative trades. Commercial trade can be defined as a trade that takes place in conjunction with an economic activity. For example, let's say that China is looking to export its goods to the United States. The United States has the option to pay for the importation of these goods via the Forex. As you can see, this transaction differs from other types of transactions that take place in other types of markets. Instead of seeking to make a profit, a commercial transaction is merely facilitating the flow of money via an exchange rate. On the other hand, a speculative transaction is one that aligns more closely with what we traditionally consider a stock market exchange. In other words, a speculative transaction is one where an individual will exchange one type of currency with another in the hope that this trade will eventually lead to greater profit, either in the short or long term.

This chapter has sought to provide a general understanding of what the Forex market is and how it differs from other types of investment strategies that are available to you. With both commercial and speculative transactions having been defined, the next chapter will be able to contextualize the current climate of the Forex market. This will allow you to better understand how the Forex works and who is primarily operating within it.

Chapter 2

Understanding Market Trends

As we just discussed in the previous chapter, there are two types of trades that can be made on the Forex. Until recently, the majority of deals that were made on the Forex were commercial in nature; however, in recent years this trend has begun to shift. This chapter will look at why more people seem to be flocking to the Forex, and will also look at the types of businesses and entities that are most commonly associated with Forex trading. In addition to learning about the key players on the Forex market, this chapter will also look at some of the key factors that influence Forex negotiations.

Speculative Trading Overtaking Commercial Trading

Before the 1970s, trading currency only comprised roughly ten percent of the world's total global trade. In other words, people were largely trading goods and services in exchange for global currency. They were not simply trading currency in exchange for a different type of currency. By the mid-1990s, this percentage exploded to include currency trading off about 1.2 trillion dollars. Additionally, it's important to understand that as interest in currency exchange grew, so did interest in speculative trading. As technology brought global economies closer to one another, people began to see that they could gain profit through the speculative trading of currencies. Economic decisions such as offshoring jobs and the rise of global banking institutions are both progressive changes in the world that led to more trade on the Forex for profit.

Who Primarily Trades Forex?

Just because there has been a rise in speculative trading does not mean that it's primarily individuals trading on the Forex, although individuals have recently become more interested in trading in this manner as well. The most prevalent entities that trade on the Forex include the following:

1. **Retail Traders:** Retail traders are those who market themselves over the internet as being a legitimate broker for providing Forex services to individuals. Since 2007, the online retail trade industry has been able to contribute to a whopping $150 billion dollars being traded on the Forex market. This number is huge, but the volatility of the Forex market itself along with the potential to be easily duped over the internet are two reasons to be extremely cautious when trading in this manner. Retail traders can also be identified as individual investors because these online retail traders are who represent an individual's Forex account.

2. **Banks:** The prevalence of banking institutions that are trading on the Forex is larger than that of the retail traders. When banks engage in activity on the Forex, they're doing so for both their

clients as well as themselves. In both cases, these are speculative deals. The bank is able to make a profit from the transaction they're negotiating for their client, as well as when they are negotiating for themselves.

3. **Central Banks:** Not to be confused with banks, central banks are national banks that control factors such as interest rates, inflation rates, and other factors related to monetary policy. A country's central bank would negotiate commercial, rather than speculative deals, on the Forex.

4. **Corporations:** Global corporations that often import and export goods to other countries would be considered commercial investors on the Forex. Whenever one country needs to pay another country, they will need to do so in the currency of the country that is being paid. This is where the Forex comes in handy.

As you can see, the majority of investors on the Forex are not individuals, but rather large businesses that have global reach and influence. It's important that you understand this as someone who is perhaps thinking about trading on the Forex yourself. Individuals will always have varying reasons for becoming interested in Forex, but the notion that you can become wealthy in this manner in your own right is becoming more popular as well. For example, perhaps you have already heard of Sandile Shezi, the 20-something who became a millionaire in South Africa because of his ability to learn and excel at trading on the Forex market. As stories like Shezi's become more prevalent and popular, the likelihood that more people will become motivated to trade currency on the Forex platform is much more likely.

Influential Forex Factors

Now that you know more about the key players on the Forex and how individual investors fit into that mix, we will now look at some of the most significant factors that can affect how the Forex market is doing at a given point in time. These factors include the following:

1. **A Country's GDP:** A country's Gross Domestic Product is one tool that a Forex investor can use in order to determine how powerful a particular economy and their currency is. When GDP for a country is calculated, it is calculated through the following equation: their entire profit for the year from what they've produced minus what their country has consumed. If a country's GDP is a large number, it means that they are able to produce more than they use. This means that they're likely able to sell their leftover goods and services to people in other parts of the world, and will be able to see even more profit in this way.

2. **Importation and Exportation:** Another factor that you want to be on the lookout for when you're considering countries in which to invest include their importation and exportation activity. When a country is importing a lot of their goods to their people, it essentially means that they're

supporting a different country financially because they have to pay this other country in order to receive the goods that they're providing. On the other hand, when a country is exporting a lot of goods to another place, it means that the country is able to produce a good or a service that another country finds attractive. You can think of exportation of a good as being similar to another country investing in another country who produces a superior good. As a money-hungry investor, you should be on the lookout for countries that export many goods to other places in the world.

3. **A Country's Unemployment Rate:** Another factor that can greatly influence an investor's decisions is a country's unemployment rate. When a country is unable to provide jobs for their citizens, the country is likely not going to be prosperous, especially from an investment perspective. Additionally, if you're noticing that the people of a particular region of the world are having to move somewhere else into to make

themselves financially stable, this should indicate that you should protect your money by avoiding this country as an investment option.

4. **Interest Rates:** The last significant Forex market factor at which we'll look are a country's currency interest rates. A country's central bank has the power to determine what a country's interest rate for their currency is going to be; however, it's important to understand that supply and demand can also naturally change a currency's interest rate if and when a central bank wants to have a more "hands-off" approach. By keeping an eye on what a country's central bank is doing in regard to a currency's interest rate, a savvy investor is able to discern the attitude that any country's government has towards investing opportunities and their currency's growth potential.

Chapter 3

Frequently-Used Terminology on the Foreign-Exchange Market

Now that you have a solid background on what the Forex is, who is trading on it, and how you can determine the health of a country's currency, it's time to get into the nitty-gritty of how Forex truly operates. This chapter is going to provide you with essential information regarding terms and concepts that you need to know if you ever hope to get good at trading on the Forex. This chapter will provide the basis for all other concepts that will be later presented in this book. With a solid foundation of terms under your belt, you will then be able to move onto learning more complex topics in regarding Forex trading.

Essential Forex Term 1: A Currency Pair and Quote

On the Forex, when a currency stands alone, it really has little value. The Forex is all about currency exchange, and this involves comparing one currency type with another. Remember, it's very unlikely that one type of currency is going to have the exact same value as another type of currency (this is largely due to the factors that were presented in the previous chapter). In order to figure out how much a currency is worth in relation to another type of currency, a currency pair is needed. A currency pair is also known as a quote because this pair is able to provide you with knowledge on how much another type of currency is worth. This makes sense when you think about other types of quotes that exist in the world. For example, if you want someone to come out and repair a broken window in your home, it's unlikely that you would want them to come do the work and then tell you how much it's going to cost. Instead, you would want them to quote you a price for the work that they're going to be doing. A currency quote works similarly. Prior to investing in a type of currency, you're going to want to know how much bang you're going to get for your buck. That's what a quote in the Forex will be able to tell you.

A few examples of the most common currency pairs that you're likely to see on the Forex are dictated below:

EUR/USD: Euro compared to US Dollar
USD/JPY: US Dollar compared to Japanese Yen
GBP/USD: British Pound compared to US Dollar
USD/CHF: US dollar compared to Swiss Franc

As you can see from the examples above, each currency type that is traded on the Forex can be shortened to a three-letter abbreviation. You can use the chart below as a reference to quickly determine the abbreviations for commonly-traded currency:

Currency	Symbol
US Dollar	USD
Swedish Krona	SEK
New Zealand Dollar	NZD
Norwegian Krone	NOK
Japanese Yen	JPY
British Pound	GBP
European Euro	EUR
Swiss Franc	CHF
Canadian Dollar	CAD
Australian Dollar	AUD

Each currency pair is going to contain what's known as a base currency and a quote currency. The base currency is always going to be on the left side of the slash symbol, while the quote currency is always going to be on the right side of the slash. What does this mean? The base currency is always going to represent 1 unit of currency. The quote currency is going to represent how much of that currency you need in order to fulfill 1 unit of the base currency.

For example, let's say that you're traveling to London soon and are interested in trading some of your US dollars with British pounds. Right now, a currency pair that would dictate how many pounds you would get for 1 US dollar would look like the following:

USD/GBP = 1.30

This currency pair tells you that if you wanted to receive British pounds for 1 US dollar, you would receive 1.3 British pounds. It's important to understand that most currency pairs on the Forex are going to be dictated in relation to the US dollar. Today, more than eighty-percent of currency trades involve the US dollar in some way. This is because of the fact that the US dollar is represented in over fifty-percent of banks all around the world. Goods that are essential to the existence of many countries are also traded with the US dollar as the base currency. These include coal, oil, and sugar, just to name a few; however, this does not mean that there are not instances where other types of currencies are compared directly with one another. Whenever two currencies that are not the US dollar are compared with one another, it's known as a cross-currency pair.

Direct Quotes versus Indirect Quotes

In addition to currency pairs and quotes, there are two sub-categories of quotes that also need to be discussed. These are known as direct and indirect quotes. The definition of both of these terms is going to depend on whether the currency with which you're dealing is your domestic currency or is an international currency. A direct quote is simply a currency pair that is quoted with your domestic currency as the quoted currency. An indirect quote is the opposite, where the international currency is the quoted currency and the domestic currency is the base.

For example, we already know that USD/GBP = 1.30. If you lived in the United States, this would be an indirect quote because the pound is the quoted currency. If you lived in London, this would be a direct quote because the

British pound is the currency that's being quoted against 1 US dollar.

Essential Forex Term 2: Exchange Rate

In the example above of the US dollar and British pound currency pair, the difference between 1 unit of the dollar and 1.30 units of the British pound is known as the exchange rate between the two currencies. This is a fairly simple concept to understand, but it's also important to understand that on the Forex, in particular, investors are interested in many numbers that come after the decimal point in a currency pair. Let's stick with the example that we already have. 1.30 British pounds has been rounded to create an even number. If in reality, this number is actually 1.3425, a Forex investor is going to want to know. When you're trading a lot of currency for another type, 1 cent could end up meaning the difference between 1 cent and 1 thousand dollars.

Essential Forex Term 3: Pips

This notion of decimals having great significance brings us to the notion of a pip. A pip can be best defined as 1/100th of a cent that is expressed in a currency pair. Another way to think of a pip is to consider it as the fourth decimal place that is quoted in a currency pair. Having pips in currency pairs makes it possible for investors to account for how much a currency is worth down to an exact amount. Additionally, another term that relates to the pip is known as the pipette. A pipette represents 1/1000th of a cent or the decimal place in a currency pair. The fact that pips and pipettes even exist as concepts should provide you with some insight into how much small fluctuations within the Forex market matter.

Essential Forex Term 4: Bid Price and Ask Price

Two other common terms that you will often see being used in conjunction with one another are the bid price and the ask price. Quite simply, the bid price is the highest price that one investor is willing to pay in order to obtain a certain amount of currency. Contrastingly, the ask price is the lowest price a seller is willing to take in order to sell a currency. These two price requirements will often dictate whether or not a sale will actually take place on the Forex.

Essential Forex Term 5: Long Position and Short Position

Two other terms that should be defined together are known as long and short positions. A long position is when an investor purchases a currency with the hope that the value of that currency is going to grow over the long-term. Contrastingly, a short position is when an investor sells a currency with the expectation that the currency is going to depreciate in value. In both instances, the investor is able to generate the most money for him or herself, if correct in their assumption.

Essential Forex Term 6: The Spread

The spread is the difference between the bid price and the ask price. Often, the spread is displayed in pips. This makes it obvious that there is often only a small difference between the bid price and the ask price; so small, in fact, that the difference is only able to be expressed in a decimal.

Essential Forex Term 7: Leverage

Leverage is when an investor borrows money with the intention of making, even more, money than they would be able to if they did not borrow money in the first place. While leveraging your money can lead to riches, it can also lead to great losses as well. Generally speaking, leveraging is a risky way to try and reap profit because when you borrow money you have to pay all of that money back and also pay any interest that is attached to it. Sure, if you're able to make this money grow than leveraging will certainly yield reward, but losing a lot of money is entirely possible with leveraging.

Essential Forex Term 8: Volatility

The last essential term we'll discuss is volatility. The entire Forex market is considered to be rather volatile because small changes in the pips can often lead to large gains and losses, but volatility most often refers to fluctuations in a single currency pair's exchange rate. If there is a lot of movement in the price of one currency pair, it's considered to be experiencing a lot of volatility.

Chapter 4

Common Chart Patterns You're Likely to See

The next step to being able to say that you fully understand the Forex market is to educate yourself on the basic types of chart patterns that exist within it. Without being able to pull information from Forex charts and graphs, you're not going to be able to accurately determine what information means. After reading this chapter, you will understand three basic chart patterns. These patterns are Double Top and Double Bottom and Head and Shoulder chart patterns. Yes, these patterns may sound foreign to you right now, but this chapter will make all of these chart patterns relatively simple to understand so that you can easily extract the information that you need from them.

Chart Type 1: Double Top and Bottom Charts

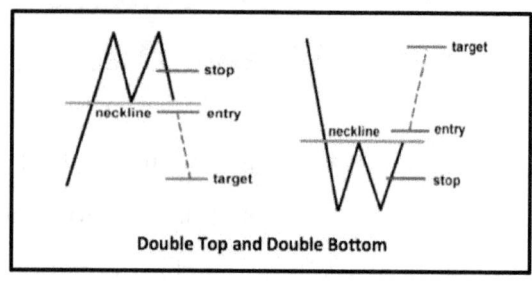

Double Top and Double Bottom

Let's start with a double top chart first. As you can see in the graph to the left above, there are two mountain-like peaks at the top of this graph. While the shapes of the mountains themselves vary slightly, these points stop at exactly the same spot. When one peak is formed on a chart, it doesn't mean much, but when two peaks are formed on a chart, it means that investors have been selling a particular currency but it cannot be sold for a higher price than what is indicated on the chart. When you see two peaks, it means that people are likely going to stop buying the currency pair in question. If an investor sees a peak like this, he or she will likely purchase this currency pair below the two peaks in the chart because he or she is anticipating that the price is going to drop soon. A depiction of this drop can be seen in the image below. Typically, investors will see a double top chart pattern and change their investment position in the short-term.

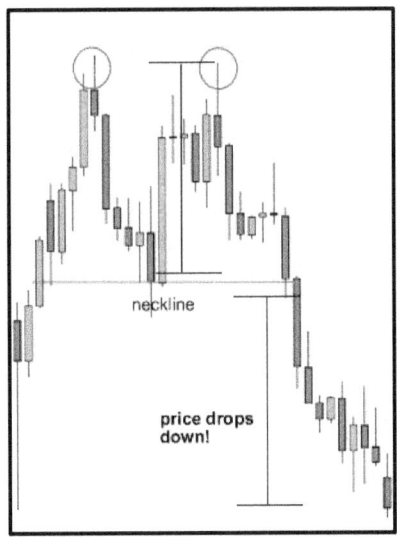

The Double Bottom Chart Pattern

In contrast to the double top chart pattern, a double bottom is one that investors will see and then change their investment strategy for the long-term. With this type of chart pattern, the same two peaks are going to be visible, but they are going to be seen towards the lower part of a chart, as seen in the image below:

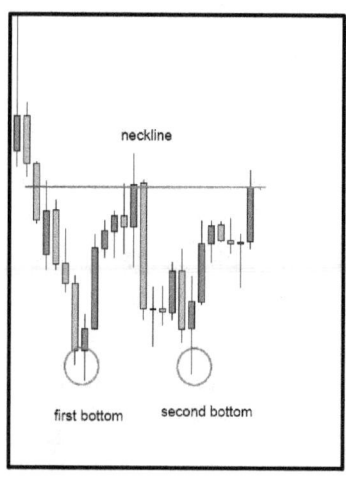

While the first bottom can indicate to an investor that an uptrend might occur, the second bottom provides enough insight that a rise in price is very likely. When a savvy investor sees this type of chart activity, he or she will likely position their investment at a price that is around the neckline in the image above. In addition to the two bottoms in the image, the neckline is also an important aspect of this chart pattern because it is able to indicate to an investor that the price of the currency has not trended past that point for some time. For this reason, keeping the price around the neckline is a good idea, at least until a greater upward trend becomes apparent.

Chart Type 2: Head and Shoulders Chart Patterns

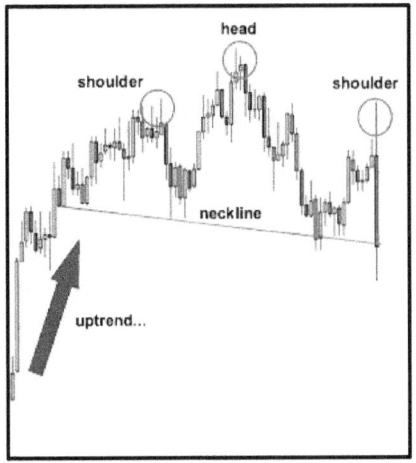

The name of the head and shoulders chart pattern relates to the three points that can be seen on it. In other words, the three points on this type of chart pattern connote an image of a person with a head and two shoulders. The head represents the single highest point on the chart, while the two shoulders represent a reversal in stock price at around equal measurement. When an investor sees a head and shoulder chart pattern, it can be discerned that the price of a share has not gone past the head point. For this reason, an investor will typically place stock in currency at a price that is below the trending neckline that can be drawn through a line between the two shoulder points on the chart. It's important to understand that even though the price may drop even further, placing an investment below the neckline is advised because it is seen as a relatively safe bet. If the price does not drop more significantly, your investment will still be safe.

An Inverse Head and Shoulders Pattern

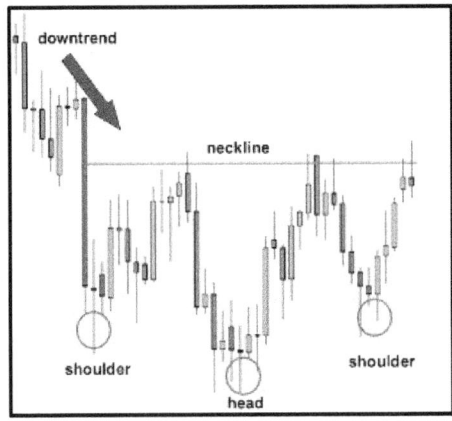

In contrast to an upright head and shoulders pattern, an inverse head and shoulders chart pattern is going to indicate that an upward movement in currency price is likely to occur. As you can see in the image above, a neckline has also been drawn between the two shoulder points on the chart. This time, instead of placing an investment below the neckline, this chart would indicate that you should place an investment above the neckline because it's likely that the currency price is going to continue to rise.

As you can see from both of the chart patterns at which we looked in this chapter, a single high or low point on a chart is not enough to indicate a particular trend on the Forex market; however, two points can often provide you with insight as to where a trend is headed. Additionally, the neckline on these two chart patterns will be able to provide you with the ability to determine where you should be setting your investment. When you're considering how much money to put on the line, it's important to keep in mind that greed can also be riskier than its worth. Stick to the advice that was presented in this chapter in regard to keeping your investment close to a chart's neckline price. This will help to prevent you from easily losing your shirt on the Forex.

Chapter 5

The Attitude You Need to Cultivate

There are plenty of strategic elements of Forex trading that you need to think about, and trading psychology is certainly one of them. Yes, there are plenty of technical elements to Forex trading, but if you don't bolster your mindset in a particular manner, understanding these technical fundamentals will likely not result in great profit. This chapter will provide you with information regarding how you can start thinking like a real and serious investor.

Conquering Your Dreams of Greed

As we've already discussed, there is certainly money that can be made on the Forex, but it's important to recognize that this potential is not the equivalent of endless wealth and easy fortune. Too many new Forex traders seem to think that if he or she makes decisions quickly, wealth is inevitable. This is not the case. Yes, any good investor is looking to make money, but when this desire to make money is confused with a need to become rich no matter what, our brain can become confused. When our brain is confused, any good trading strategy can become reckless and unfocused.

To combat the sneaky voice of greed in our head, it's best to stay disciplined in your trading approach whenever possible. Don't worry, the next chapter is going to discuss some basic trading strategies that you can use for yourself. For now, keep in mind that being disciplined when you trade is perhaps the most important factor that any investor, new or old, should learn to cultivate if they want to ever see a frequent profit. Too often do investors become impatient in their trading approach. When you don't give your strategy enough time to develop, success becomes much less likely.

Trade Emotionlessly

In conjunction with feelings of greed that can sometimes latch onto our psyche while trading, emotions are another factor that can dictate a trading situation without us even realizing it. For example, if you get attached to a favorable outcome that you're seeing through a particular currency share, it can become more difficult to let go of that share when it is no longer suiting your portfolio. This is where developing a strategy and sticking with it no matter what can come in handy. By thinking of your strategy as being paramount to any emotional attachment that you have to a particular share, you will be able to think more objectively about how to grow your money.

Fear versus Conservatism

In opposition to greed, fear is another type of problem that can arise in our psyche when we're not devout in our trading strategy. While greed can prompt someone to make a hasty decision, fear is greed's pesky cousin who seems to never be able to make a solid decision. To compensate for the possibilities of fear, the first step is to continuously remind yourself that you are in control of your trading destiny. In any type of stock market, chance is not something that holds weight. The tools that you're going to be using for stock analysis are what should be driving you to make certain decisions. Sometimes this analysis will lead you to profit, while other times this analysis will lead you to a loss, even when you're sure that your analysis was correct. This is simply the nature of the stock market. When you defy your analysis and act in a fearful manner instead of in a manner that you know to be empirically correct, you're putting yourself in a losing position mentally.

In contrast to fear, there are plenty of conservative Forex investors out there. There's nothing wrong with that. A conservative investor is someone who is doubtful of any information that he or she receives, and will often not decide until he or she can verify this information with empirical data. If you know that you're more conservative in your trading practices, stick with this strategy. Do not confuse it with fear. It's okay to be conservative, as long as you know when to pull the trigger.

Why Are You Entering the Forex Market?

Prior to entering the Forex market, you need to ask yourself why you're choosing to do so. Asking yourself this question is going to help you to combat the feelings of greed and fear that are prevalent in Forex trading psychology. Similar to any other stock market that exists, the Forex market should not be considered an avenue that is going to lead to quick riches. If you want to make money in this manner, you're going to have to work for it and study your craft. A good way to figure out why you're choosing to enter the Forex market is to set a monthly monetary goal for yourself. Another tactic that you can use is to consider if you're going to use the profit from Forex trading for any savings goal. Do you have a kid who's going to need a college fund? Do you want to start seriously saving for retirement? Do you want to purchase a larger house than the one that you currently have? Each investor's exact circumstances will differ, but if you don't understand why you're in the market, setting goals for yourself will prove difficult.

Making decisions based on an emotion like greed is one of the most common mistakes that an investor can make when it comes to developing a foundational trading mindset. The best way to combat any emotional or psychological setbacks that you may face, especially when you're first starting to trade Forex, is to develop a strict trading strategy for yourself. By refusing to succumb to your emotions, you're going to be able to make objective decisions that can be based on the charts that you're referencing, or the news that you're watching about a particular country's currency during a given point in time. Remember, in the Forex market (and any other investment market) chance as a reason for planning is not considered valid.

Chapter 6

Beginner Strategies to Make You a Buck

Now that we've gone over the mindset that you need to cultivate in order to see success as a Forex trader, we are now going to look at some strategies that can help you to become more disciplined and strategic. This way, you will be able to achieve your strategic goals. There are two strategies that this book is going to focus on, which are known as the carry trade strategy and the SMA strategy. After reading this chapter, you will understand what each strategy is as well as how to implement each one properly.

The Pillars of the Carry Trade Strategy

The carry trade strategy has been around since the 1980s and can be considered a moderate strategy that is able to yield an investor average returns over the long-term. The general premise surrounding this strategy is to be able to recognize differences between the interest rates of various currencies that you're considering trading. In addition to noticing when one currency has a higher interest rate than another and being able to benefit from this difference, another aspect of this strategy involves anticipating when an increase or decrease in an interest rate is going to occur.

Tactic 1 for Carry Trade: Buy Currency with the Higher Interest Rate

The first tactic that you can use when you're looking to implement a carry trade strategy is to purchase currency with a higher interest rate than the currency that you're holding. When you buy currency with a higher interest rate, you have to sell your currency with the lower interest rate, since every currency deal on the Forex requires a currency pair trade of some type. When you purchase currency in this manner, you're able to reap the profit from the difference between the low-interest currency that you're selling and the higher-interest currency that you're buying.

Tactic 2 for Carry Trade: Anticipate Interest Rate Fluctuations

Being able to profit from a difference between interest rates may seem pretty straightforward, but being able to anticipate when these fluctuations between interest rates are going to occur is a much more difficult task. You can certainly use the tactic of following a trend that you may see on the market when other investors using the carry-trade strategy, but you're always going to make less money when you're not the first investor to do something. Instead of following someone else's lead, a better way to anticipate a change in interest rate would be to pay attention to the influential market factors that we already went over in Chapter 2. You can keep track of the activity of certain interest rates by simply subscribing to news outlets that focus on the activity of certain types of currency around the world. Some resources that document this type of information include the following online resources:

1. Forex Factory
2. BabyPips
3. DailyFX
4. RatesFX
5. Traders Laboratory

Tactic 3 for Carry Trade: Keep Your Risk in Check

Capitalizing on currencies with opposing interest rates may seem pretty straightforward, but there are still legitimate risks to account for when you're trading with this strategy in mind. Most notably, there is always going to be the possibility that the interest rate of the lower currency is going to rise quickly. If it does, your profit margin is going to decrease. A great way to combat this type of risk is to make sure that the currencies that you're trading are at opposite ends of the interest rate spectrum. If the interest rates for the currencies that you're trading are too close together, there is a greater chance that you will end up losing money if the lower interest rate ends up spiking upwards or the higher interest rate ends up dropping. Using the chart patterns we already went over will also help to diminish the risk that's involved with the carry trade strategy.

All About the SMA Strategy

SMA is an acronym. When taken apart, it stands for Simple Moving Average. The goal of the SMA strategy is to be able to see the average price of a currency pair over a certain period of time. The equation that you can use to calculate a simple moving average can be seen below:

Pair Price + Pair Price + Pair Price / Certain Period of Time

Let's make this equation more straightforward with an example. You're interested in trading your Japanese Yen for US dollars. You're pretty sure that you can make a profit from this type of exchange, but you want to be conservative in your efforts. You decide that calculating the SMA for US dollars will allow you to reach your profit goals while still being conservative. Over the past three days, the closing pair price of the US dollar in relation to the Japanese Yen has been the following:

Day 1: USD/JPY = 3.50

Day 2: USD/JPY = 3.20

Day 3: USD/JPY = 3.25

To calculate the SMA for these three days, all you would have to do is add up these three numbers and then divide by 3. This would give you an SMA of 3.31667. Once you have your SMA calculated, it does not mean that you should invest based on the number that you've derived. This is because the SMA is better utilized as something that can provide you with a long-term analysis of how this currency pair has performed in the past. Instead of using the SMA strategy to invest immediately after it's calculated, it's advised that you calculate the SMA for a currency pair frequently prior to making any conclusions about how this currency pair will perform in the future. Savvy investors will calculate a range of SMA figures over a long duration, in order to see trends that cannot be ascertained without their SMA calculations.

Crossover SMA

In addition to a traditional use of the Simple Moving Average, some investors also choose to use the SMA as a way to determine when they should buy and sell additional pairs of that currency. First, the investor would calculate the SMA over the long-term of the currency pair's past. This way, the investor knows the history of this currency pair and its pattern of interest rate activity. Next, the investor would track the SMA of this currency pair over a more recent period of time. After both of these averages have been calculated, the investor can then set a point where he or she will know that it's time to buy or sell more of this stock. This is similar to the neckline that we saw in the chapter regarding chart patterns. In this way, the investor can choose a distinct price that will determine his or her investment activity. The crossover SMA strategy is not only useful for strategic purposes; it can also help to steer you away from making an emotional investment because you have put in place a concrete way of determining how you will buy and sell a particular currency pair.

Chapter 7

Online Tools Every New Forex Trader Should Use

In addition to having some fool-proof strategies at your disposal, another important aspect of the Forex investment process is having tools that you can use to accelerate and enhance your investment progress. The rise of the internet has made Forex trading easier and more efficient than ever before. For this reason, it's important that you become aware of the tools that will be presented in this chapter. Many investors rely heavily on the tools that the internet can provide. Without being aware of what these tools can offer your investment strategy, you will find yourself at a significant disadvantage.

The Evolution of Technology

Before we start discussing the tools that you need to have in order to consider yourself a reputable Forex investor, it's important to understand why you should be considering these online tools at all. The most significant reason why you should be considering online trading tools is that, in the recent past, you would have been unable to make decisions through an online platform at all. Instead, you would have been forced to call a broker each and every time you were looking to make a decision in relation to your Forex portfolio. With the technology that is available today, you're able to feel as if you're truly in control of your investment strategy and the pace with which this strategy is implemented.

Before We Get to Digital Tools…

While digital tools are definitely important because they can expedite the Forex researching process, there is still one tool that has been used for ages since Forex trading began. This tool is a journal. A journal does not have to be digital in nature, although it certainly can be. You should consider documenting the following information for every potential transaction you're thinking about making on the Forex:

1. **Your Trading Intention:** Remember, when you're trading on the Forex, nothing should be motivated by chance. For this reason, you should be thinking about your motivation for considering a certain deal prior to doing so. While you may have a vague idea in your head about why you're planning to make a particular decision, physically writing it down will allow you to make sure that your intentions are grounded in objective, rather than emotional reasons.

2. **Your Strategy:** Once you've determined that you're definitely going to move forward with a particular investment decision, the next thing to document in your journal is how you're going to strategize and achieve monetary gain. In addition to documenting the specific strategy that you're going to be using, it would also be a good idea to also document the exact buy-in or sell-out price you're going to target.

3. **How Large Will Your Position Be?** Once you have determined how you're going to initiate a particular investment based on the strategy that you've developed in relation to your goals, the next step is to determine how much money you're going to risk. The amount that you're going to put on the line should be determined by how aggressive your investment strategy is.

In addition to making sure that you're documenting these three important considerations, you should also make it a point to include any feelings that might arise as you move through trading Forex. It's normal to feel a certain way about the investments that you're making, just as long as you don't allow these feelings to dictate your decisions. In addition to documenting your feelings, it would also be a good idea to document any mistakes that you make along the way. Regardless of what someone may tell you, everyone who trades on any market has made plenty of mistakes while in pursuit of earning their dough. You're no different. By keeping track of the mistakes that you make along the way, you'll be much less likely to make them again in the future.

You'll Need Charting Software

After you've decided how you're going to keep your journal (either in a Word document or with a paper and pen) the next tool that you're going to need is excellent charting software. While the basic stock market charts will be able to provide you with an overview of what's going on within the Forex market, charting software has algorithms embedded within it that will enable you to see things that you'd otherwise miss. These subtleties are known as "indicators". Some common indicators that will come with any good charting software include the following:

1. Bollinger Bands
2. Stochastic RSI
3. Fibonacci Sequence

Getting into the details of each of these indicators is beyond the scope of this book; however, it's still important for you to make sure that the charting software that you ultimately purchase is able to provide you with indicators such as these. Additionally, the best charting software on the market right now includes the following products:

1. MetaTrader 4 or MetaTrader 5
2. eSignal
3. ProRealTime
4. MetaStock
5. TradingView

An Economic Calendar

When you're trading on the Forex, you're also going to need an economic calendar. This tool will help you to keep yourself in check with the volatility that is integral to the Forex. Another reason why an economic calendar is important is that it will allow you to track Fundamental Announcements that take place within the market. Also known as "Fundys", these announcements often pertain to ones regarding changing interest rates, unemployment reports, or information about banks in various countries. When these announcements are made, you'll be able to track them on your calendar and thus understand the periods of potential volatility that result from these types of announcements with more clarity.

A Time Zone Adjuster

Another essential Forex tool is one that will adjust your time zones for you. Think about it – if you own currency that is not used within the time zone in which you live, it's unlikely that you will be able to naturally keep track when this particular market is open and trading your currency. Additionally, it's also possible for two Forex markets to be open and trading at the same time. This means that if you have invested in currency in both of these locations, you're going to need to keep an eye on two markets simultaneously. This is where a time zone adjuster tool can be useful. Most of the time, you do not even have to pay for this type of adjustment tool. Simply type something along the lines of, "time zone converter for Forex" into Google and you should be able to find what you're looking for.

A Currency Volatility Chart

Lastly, a currency volatility chart is going to provide you with information regarding how volatile certain currencies are, and when they're expected to most volatile. You can see an example of what a currency volatility chart will look like below:

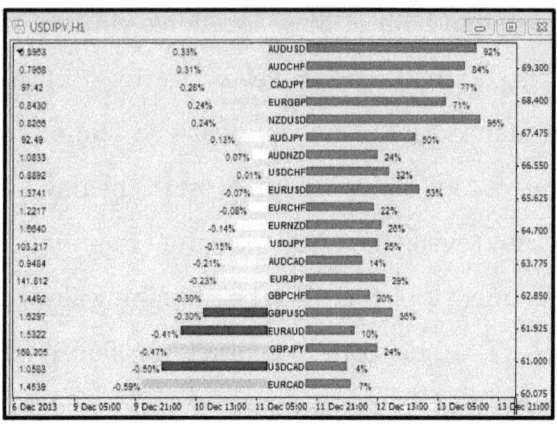

The tools that were presented in this chapter should be considered essential items that will help you to grow your Forex endeavors to new levels. Without these tools, you're not going to be able to make sound investment decisions. These types of tools can offer you speed and accuracy that is simply not possible when you're only relying on your own mathematical prowess. If you want to become a competitive Forex investor, you also have to invest in the tools that will aid in your success.

Chapter 8

Three Different Forex Markets from Which You Can Trade

There are three broad market types that exist within the Forex. This chapter will go into each of these three market types in detail. The three types of markets that exist within Forex include the following:

1. The Futures Market
1. The Spot Market
2. The Forwards Market

While you may eventually get to a point where you feel comfortable and confident in investing in multiple Forex market-types simultaneously, when you're first starting to learn how to trade on the Forex, it's recommended that you stick to investing in just one market type. Let's take a look at each of these market types in detail now.

Information Regarding the Futures Market

The futures market can be best described as a subcategory of the Forex market that focuses on negotiating currency deals through contracts. The most important piece of information that you should know about the Futures market is that two people alone cannot engage in this type of deal. Instead, the Futures market is monitored by an entity known as the National Futures Association. In this type of market, currency is traded between multiple interested parties at the same time, and the National Futures Association acts an administrator and mediator for these contracts to take place. Many investors see the Futures market to be one of the avenues of Forex investing that is particularly stringent in nature. These types of transactions are also going to be larger than ones that exist in the other two types of markets that we have yet to discuss. For this reason, they will also usually take longer to implement.

Information Regarding the Spot Market

Unlike the Futures market that has relatively long wait times, the Spot market is primarily focused on the here and now. In other words, investors within the Spot market are going to be looking at how currency pairs are doing in real-time, and they will typically quickly pay in cash when they see a currency pair in which they'd like to invest. Specifically, the investor who is selling the currency pair will provide the quoted currency, while the person who is looking to purchase the share will do so with the pair's base currency. Even though the Spot market is all about making investment decisions "on the spot", investors are also able to see how a stock, in particular, is predicted to do in the future. Generally speaking, a Spot market deal is going to take around two days to process. This type of market does not typically work within contracts.

Information Regarding the Forwards Market

Similar to the Futures market, the Forwards market does use contracts when negotiating investments; however, unlike the Futures market, the Forwards market is not monitored by any overarching entity. It's best to think of the Forwards market as being in the middle of a formality because it's more formal than the Spot market but less formal than the Futures market. In a Forwards market contract, both the seller and the buyer are going to agree upon a price for which the currency pair will be bought and sold. Once these two parties agree upon a price, the outcome of this agreement can change, depending on market volatility. In other words, prior to the contract being signed and completed, the seller is hoping that the exchange rate for this currency pair will increase in value so that he or she can make more of a profit from this contract. Contrastingly, the buyer is hoping that the exchange rate for this currency pair will decrease in value so that he or she will have to pay less for this pair. As you can see, the buyer and the seller will often have opposing desires within this market in particular.

Which Market Should You Choose

When you're first beginning to trade on the Forex, it's advised that you do so through the Forwards market. As we've already stated, this is the hybrid market when it comes to strictness, and this market also has a faster turnaround time than does the Futures market, but a slower turnaround time compared to the Spot market. This means that you will feel less pressured to negotiate a deal than you would within the Spot market, but will also be able to negotiate more quickly than you would be able to within the Futures market. This will allow you to make decisions that are objective without feeling too pressured to make any irrational choices. Remember, even if you don't end up feeling like the Forwards market is for you when you're first starting out in the Forex, choosing only one of these markets is essential. You need to learn how to master one of these markets first, before attempting to figure out another one. If you don't take your time within each one and learn each one separately, the chances of confusing the regulations within each one are much more likely.

Chapter 9

All About Stop Loss Orders

In addition to understanding the three different types of markets from which you can choose to invest on the Forex, understanding how to use a stop loss order is also crucial to your overall success. While some people may perceive the stop loss order to be a small detail in relation to the entire Forex platform, stop loss orders are also considered by many veteran investors to be essential to any legitimate and competitive trading strategy. With many investors regarding the stop loss order as being highly important to their goals as Forex investors, it's important that you understand what a stop loss order can offer your trading strategy as well.

Defining the Stop Loss Order

At its core, a stop loss order is a tool that can prevent you from losing a large sum of money, if and when the currency in which you've invested drops dramatically in value. To implement a stop loss order, your broker will need to be involved. Basically, you let your broker know the specific price you'd like to set your stop loss order at. What this means is that if the price of your currency pair dips below a particular price, your investment will not be affected. For example, let's say that you recently bought a share of Japanese Yen and it's currently worth $1.20 US dollars. Even though you're currently happy that your Yen is worth more than 1 US dollar unit, your research is showing you that the Yen is likely to fall in value very soon. You're a rather conservative investor. You're also not emotionally invested in any of the deals that you make. For these reasons, in order to prevent any significant loss in profit, you decide that you will only be willing to lose up to ten percent of this investment that you've made in Yen. Once you've made this decision, you contact your broker. At this point, he or she is going to place a stop loss order at $1.08. This means that if the Yen drops below $1.08, you are only going to have lost 12 cents on your investment.

The Benefits and Pitfalls of a Stop Loss Order

In addition to being able to prevent yourself from losing large sums of money, another primary advantage that a stop loss order can provide is that it allows you to spend less time monitoring your money. When you put a stop loss order in place, you can feel comfortable knowing that you've already set up the maximum amount you're willing to lose ahead of time. This is also a great planning feature because it means that you've taken the time to predetermine what your maximum loss will be.

While the benefits of a stop loss order are great, nothing in the world of investing comes without a potential consequence. Stop loss orders are no different. The primary pitfall of the stop loss order is the fees that go with this type of transaction. Obviously, your broker is going to want something in return for implementing this type of strategy for you. While a broker's fee for implementing a stop loss order for you should be reasonable, if you fall into the habit of putting a stop loss order in place prematurely or too often, these commission costs are going to add up quickly. Some investors make the grave mistake of not watching their commission costs closely. If you're placing many stop loss orders and not accounting for commission costs, you could end up losing more money than the stop loss orders are worth in the first place. Remember, every transaction on the Forex market has a cost associated with it. If you're not careful, these costs will end up costing you all of the profit that you've seen, and then some.

A good way to combat the potential transaction fees that go along with stop loss orders is to first make sure that the stop loss order that you're placing is one that can be used over the long term. For example, if you know that a particular currency pair is particularly volatile, it's advised that you do not place a stop loss order if you're only going to retract this order shortly thereafter. If you do feel as though a stop loss order is an appropriate measure to take, even if you know the position of the currency pair is volatile, then it's highly advised that you place your stop loss order with this potential volatility in mind.

For example, if you already know that the currency pair in question typically fluctuates by over ten percent in a given week, then it would make little sense to place a stop loss order at only a six percent or seven percent point of loss. While the specific circumstances surrounding your stop loss order are going to vary, the basic point is that you should calculate your stop loss order based on the history of volatility for the particular currency pair with which you're dealing.

Chapter 10

How to Manage Your Risk Like a Winner

After you've figured out a general strategy from which to dictate your Forex trading goals, there is still work to do. Any adequate trading strategy is going to have some sort of risk management strategy in place as well, as this will help to stabilize any basic Forex strategy that you put into place. Specifically, this chapter is going to cover how you can mathematically determine your risk/reward ratio, how you should be thinking about the frequency of your returns, and how you can go about avoiding risking too much of your earnings and total investment money.

How to Determine the Risk-Reward Ratio for a Given Transaction

A risk-reward ratio is not a definitive equation that you can apply to every transaction that you're considering; however, it is still a handy tool that you can use when you're thinking about the security of your potential investment. To calculate a risk-reward ratio, first, you need to think about the amount of money that you're looking to make a given investment. Once you have this number in mind, the next step is to multiply it by the maximum risk percentage that you'd be okay potentially losing. To solidify this concept, let's look at an example.

You have your eyes set on a currency pair between US dollars and Canadian dollars. You believe that the market is ripe for profit to be gained. After doing your preliminary research and using your online tools as your guide, you believe that you could potentially gain a $9,000 profit if you play your cards right. You're excited about the potential of this investment, but also do not want to put yourself into a situation where you lose all of your money. To compensate for this legitimate worry, you decide to utilize the principles of the risk reward ratio.

With $9,000 being your profit goal, the next step is to think about the maximum percentage you're willing to lose if something were to go wrong with this transaction. To do this, simply begin calculating how much money you would lose if the exchange rate between the Canadian dollar and the US dollar were to drastically change. You can see some of these calculations below:

50% Loss of Your Investment = $9,000 *.50 = $4,500
10% Loss of Your Investment = $9,000 * .10 = $900
5% Loss of Your Investment = $9,000 * .05 = $450

After looking at these various ratios, you ultimately decide that you're only willing to risk ten percent of your entire investment. Understanding this provides you with the ability to work within a range of risk that you can set for yourself through a concrete number. Saying to yourself, "I only want to risk up to ten percent of my total investment potential" is often less clear than saying, "I can only risk up to $900 and still feel comfortable."

Let Go of Setting Return Goals

It's not uncommon for certain investors to set small goals for themselves throughout the week or even throughout the day, depending on their individual investment frequency. While you can certainly aim to make a certain amount of money within a given time period, these types of goals are more than likely only going to put more stress on yourself. Instead of focusing on the exact amount of money that is being accumulated in the short-term, it will always be more beneficial for you to focus your energy on maintaining a certain level of discipline in relation to your investment strategy. Of course, some investors who have been trading on the Forex for quite some time will set monetary goals for themselves, but when you're first starting out doing this will likely only cause you to feel discouraged and frustrated. It's important to focus on the positive when you're first starting on the Forex.

Never Risk it All

In addition to calculating a risk-reward ratio with which you're comfortable, it's also important that you resist the urge to spend all your money within a short period of time. In fact, it's been proven that people who take on large risk over the short-term on the Forex market are more than likely going to see big losses over the long-term. For this reason, you should always be focusing more of your energy on developing a solid long-term strategy, rather than developing a short term strategy that may or may not result in large profit.

The 1% Rule

The last concept that this book will discuss is the 1% rule. This is a technique that has helped many investors keep their spending in check. To implement the 1% rule, all you have to do is count up how much money you have in the bank, and then take 1% of it. This 1% is the total amount of capital that you will allow yourself to invest on the Forex. Being strict with yourself in regards to this 1% figure, regardless of how large or how small it is, will help you to not only keep your risk in check but also help you to become a more disciplined investor as well.

Conclusion

Thank you for reading Day Trading Forex : Escape the 9 to 5 and Retire Early: Learn Essential Forex Day Trading Skills. The Basics of Currency Trading Explained in Simple Terms. Tools, Software, Tactics, Money Management, Discipline, Strategies, and Trading Psychology. Hopefully, this book has been able to provide you with sound information regarding all of the basics when it comes to Forex trading and the Forex market. At this point, you should feel ready to take on the Forex market in some capacity, whether it be simply to practice on an online platform or tackle the market in real-time.

The best advice that this book can offer you is to definitely take the time to familiarize yourself with Forex market practices in real time before you spend any of your money. Remember, the Forex market is extremely volatile, especially when compared to other types of stock markets on which you can invest. By attempting to get to know the market prior to investing anything, you will likely be able to save yourself time, money and frustration. Take your time, learn to develop a winning attitude towards the Forex market, and forge ahead. If you stick with it, you will likely see results sooner than you may initially think.

Finally, if you feel like this book was a beneficial read, let other people know! A review on Amazon is always appreciated. Thank you!

Description

Are you exhausted each day working that 9 to 5 job? We all have responsibilities that require that we make money, and yet sometimes it can seem like another day at the daily grind is just no longer possible. If you're looking for a much-needed change, look no further. Day Trading Forex can help you escape the 9 to 5 and Retire Early. In this book you will learn essential day trading Forex Skills. The Basics of Currency Trading Explained in Simple Terms. Tools, Software, Tactics, Money Management, Discipline, Strategies, and Trading Psychology. Buy right now to start educating yourself about how you can quit your boring 9 to 5 job and lead a more meaningful and lavish life. Don't follow the trend of being miserable. Breaking away from your typical job starts by picking up this book.

Imagine a life where you call the shots. You're the boss when it comes to dictating how and when you're going to live your life. When you dedicate yourself to learning about how the Forex trading market operates, you're going to find that creating a life that you truly command is easier than ever before. Yes, the Forex market is one of the riskier markets in which you can invest, but that's what makes the rewards so potentially satisfying and great. Why would you allow yourself to stay stuck in a job that isn't right for you? By reading this book, you will fully understand the attitude and discipline that you need to cultivate in order to be your best (and wealthiest) self.

This book is going to cover the following topics:

- What Forex trading is all about
- How to read Forex charts and understand Forex jargon in simple terms
- Discuss what it takes to make money in the Forex market
- Provide you with online tools that you can use to grow as an investor

- Help you to understand various beginner Forex strategies
- Educate you on why stop loss orders are so important

This book is going to provide you with all of this information and then some! There's nothing to lose. Purchasing this book immediately to start the journey towards a new and exciting career path!

www.ingramcontent.com/pod-product-compliance
Lightning Source LLC
Chambersburg PA
CBHW070312230526
45470CB00002B/846